GRAND TRAVERSE BAY

by Leah Kaminski

CHERRY LAKE PUBLISHING • ANN ARBOR, MICHIGAN

Published in the United States of America by:

CHERRY LAKE PRESS

2395 South Huron Parkway, Suite 200, Ann Arbor, MI 48104
www.cherrylakepublishing.com

Reading Adviser: Marla Conn MS, Ed., Literacy specialist, Read-Ability, Inc.

Series Adviser: Amy Reese, Coordinator of Elementary Science; Howard County School System, MD; President of Maryland Science Supervisors Association

Book Design: Book Buddy Media

Photo Credits: ©Mai Vu/Getty Images, background (pattern), ©Northern Way of Life/Shutterstock, cover (front top), ©Mark Kostich/Getty Images, cover (bottom left), ©mariusFM77/Getty Images, cover (bottom right), ©iStockphoto/ Getty Images, cover (lined paper), ©Rainer Lesniewski/Getty Images, cover (map), ©Pixabay, cover (red circle), ©Devanath/Pixabay, (paperclips), ©louanapires/Pixabay, (paper texture), ©Doug Lemke/Shutterstock, 1, ©EEI_Tony/ Getty Images, 3 (bottom left), ©Azure-Dragon/Getty Images, 3 (bottom right), ©Northern Way of Life/Shutterstock, 4, ©digidreamgrafix/Shutterstock, 6, ©Hey Darlin/Getty Images, 7, ©Crystal Eye Studio/Shutterstock, 8, ©Kirk Hewlett/ Shutterstock, 9, ©ehrlif/Shutterstock, 10, ©Bernt Rostad/Wikimedia, 12, ©Gary Richard Ennis/Shutterstock, 13, ©moose henderson/Getty Images, 14, ©DanBachKristensen/Getty Images, 15, ©Jens Domschky/Getty Images, 16, ©James Brey/Getty Images, 17, ©CT757fan/Getty Images, 18, ©emer1940/Getty Images, 19, ©Yaman Mutart/Shutterstock, 20, ©liveslow/Getty Images, 21 (top), ©aijaphoto/Shutterstock, 21 (bottom), ©Maksymowicz/Getty Images, 22, ©Wendy Piersall/Flickr, 23, ©Africa Studio/Shutterstock, 24, ©Gary Richard Ennis/Shutterstock, 25, ©simplycmb/Getty Images, 26, ©Chatchai Limjareon/Getty Images, 27, ©GlobalP/Getty Images, 28, ©EEI_Tony/Getty Images, cover (back)

Library of Congress Cataloging-in-Publication Data has been filed and is available at catalog.loc.gov

Cherry Lake Publishing would like to acknowledge the work of the Partnership for 21st Century Learning, a Network of Battelle for Kids. Please visit *http://www.battelleforkids.org/networks/p21* for more information.

Printed in the United States of America
Corporate Graphics

CONTENTS

CHAPTER 1

The Systems of Grand Traverse Bay

Grand Traverse Bay cuts into the northeastern arm of Lake Michigan. Lake Michigan is one of the five Great Lakes of North America. These lakes are freshwater seas in the center of the continent. To understand the bay, we can look at its systems. Two of these systems are its **geosphere**, or land, and its **biosphere**, or plants and animals. Other systems are its **hydrosphere**, or water, and its **atmosphere**, or weather.

Grand Traverse Bay is long and narrow. The Leelanau **Peninsula** is to its west. The narrow Mission Peninsula juts into the bay. This peninsula divides the bay into an East Arm and a West Arm. The Great Lakes were formed by *glaciers* around 14,000 years ago. The glaciers created deep valleys as they moved. Water filled the valleys when the glaciers melted. In Grand Traverse, the moving ice formed long and narrow lakes. They look like fingers on a hand. Some of these "fingers" are the East and West Arms of Grand Traverse Bay. Another finger is Elk Lake, which feeds into the bay.

The clear waters of Grand Traverse Bay are calm and welcoming to plants, animals, and humans alike.

Grand Traverse Bay is one of the few remaining oligotrophic bays in the Great Lakes. Oligotrophic means the water has a lot of **oxygen** but not a lot of **nutrients**. Oligotrophic water is clear and blue. It is also very cold. Grand Traverse has the highest water quality of Lake Michigan bays. Grand Traverse Bay is very long and points to the north. Water mostly flows into the bay from north to south. Winds blowing from the north help water and **sediment** exit the bay from south to north. The water is an average of 180 feet (55 meters) deep. Some parts are as deep as almost 600 feet (183 m).

The climate of Grand Traverse Bay affects its water. Rain and snow fall on the bay directly. They also fall on land and run into rivers and the bay. In autumn and spring, wind mixes the bay's water. The mixing combines oxygen-rich, nutrient-poor water with water that has less oxygen and more nutrients. This is called turnover.

Lake-Effect Snow

Lake-effect snow is common in Grand Traverse Bay. In fall and winter, cold air from the north crosses the waters of Lake Michigan. The air is colder than the water. The water's warmth and moisture rises into the atmosphere. Warm, moist air forms snow clouds. The snow clouds can drop 2 to 3 inches (5 to 7.6 centimeters) of snow per hour on the coast.

Winter weather freezes the upper layer of water into ice. The layers of the lake do not mix during the winter months. This is because they are different **densities**. In spring, the upper layer warms faster than the deeper layer.

Grand Traverse Bay is home to hundreds of native plants and animals. Some are only found in this region. There are many habitats in the area. Some of these habitats are inland lakes and streams, islands and reefs, rich **conifer** swamps, and dunes. Every habitat serves a purpose. Coastal **wetlands** filter sediment. Rocky reefs around islands protect small fish. Streams host insects and **spawning** fish. Every habitat is connected with others. And every sphere interacts with the others to create this lively, healthy bay.

CHAPTER 2

The Grand Traverse Bay Watershed

A watershed is the area of land that drains into a body of water. The watershed of Grand Traverse Bay includes the bay's two peninsulas. It also includes the **mainland**. The watershed provides most of the bay's water. Grand Traverse Bay receives 220 billion gallons (833 million cubic m) of water per year.

Watershed Diagram

The Grand Traverse Bay watershed is 976 square miles (2,528 square kilometers). It has 132 miles (212 km) of shoreline. All the water of this land drains into the waters of the bay.

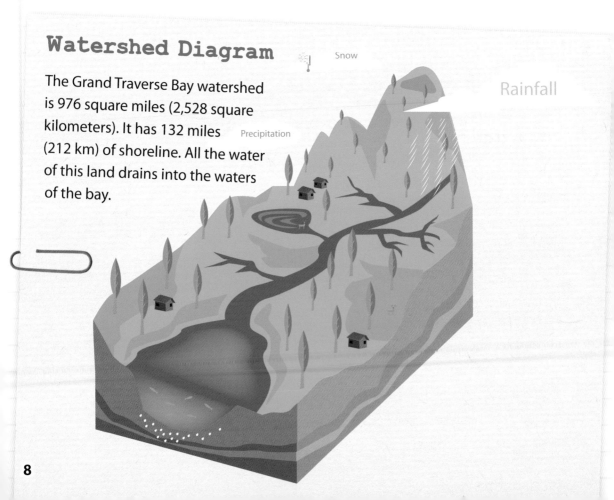

Snow

Rainfall

Precipitation

✳ The West Arm of Grand Traverse Bay can be seen from the Old Mission Peninsula, which juts into the center of the Bay.

Only around 35 percent of the bay's water comes from rain or snow falling directly on the bay. Around 60 percent comes from the watershed's rivers. Some comes from rain that soaks into the ground of the watershed. This becomes groundwater and trickles into the bay.

The watershed can affect how clean the bay's water is. Rain falls on land and soaks into the ground. The ground filters and cleans the water. Then the water flows into the bay. The rivers carry good nutrients to the bay. However, these rivers can also carry **contaminants** from human activities. The watershed is important to the bay's plants and animals, too. Rivers provide passage for birds, insects, and fish.

⁎ Human activity on the land and coast, such as piers and harbors, can bring contaminants into the bay.

There are nine parts of the Grand Traverse Bay watershed. Some are the Mitchell, Acme, Yuba, and Petobego Creeks. Others are the East and West Bay shorelines, and the Old Mission Peninsula. Two sections are the most important. These are called the Boardman River and the Elk River Chain of Lakes. The Elk River Chain of Lakes delivers almost twice as much water as the Boardman River. There are also other small rivers that flow into the bay.

The Elk River is the final, short river in the Elk River Chain of Lakes. It is only 1.5 miles (2.4 km) long.

* The Boardman River and its many streams are home to plants and animals. When the water is healthy, so are the habitats in and around it.

The Elk River Chain of Lakes is 55 miles (89 km) long. Fourteen lakes are connected by rivers. The chain ends at the bay. This part of the Grand Traverse watershed covers 500 square miles (1,295 sq km). Torch Lake is Michigan's second largest inland lake. It is also the longest.

The Boardman River flows into the bay's West Arm. It is about half the size of the Elk River Chain of Lakes area. The Boardman River begins in a swamp. It has 22 small streams that branch off of it. These are called its **tributaries**. The health of these rivers and the surrounding land is connected to the health of the bay.

CHAPTER 3

Plants and Animals of Grand Traverse Bay

Many fascinating plants and animals live in Grand Traverse Bay. Many birds use the bay for food and shelter. Coastal wetlands host two dozen bird species. Loons gather on the open water in summer. They eat small fish and amphibians. Sandpipers and plovers eat worms and snails from mud on the shore. Red-headed woodpeckers and black-throated green warblers live in forests. Gull Island is the summer home of thousands of herring gulls. Bald eagle, osprey, and northern goshawk nest in rich conifer swamps. In shrub thickets, American woodcock and ruffed grouse eat alder seeds and catkins. Humans have many farms and orchards around the bay. Cherries are the most important **crop**.

* Rare birds of prey like the bald eagle eat and sometimes nest in the wetlands of the bay.

Brook trout are native to Michigan. They lay eggs in the fall. Their eggs must have healthy water rich in oxygen and low in sediment to survive.

About 39 species of fish live in the bay. The Boardman River has been named a "Blue Ribbon" trout stream. It is filled with brook trout. Brook trout is Michigan's state fish. Other fish use the rivers of the watershed to spawn. Some of these are lake trout, sturgeon, walleye, and yellow perch. Another important fish in the area is Lake Michigan cisco. Cisco swim in large schools. About 50 years ago, Lake Michigan lost most of its cisco. Overfishing and loss of habitat killed most of these fish. The population is rebounding now. Diporeia is a tiny shrimp-like animal. It lives in sediment at the bottom of the bay. It is very important to the **food web**. Many larger fish eat it. The number of diporeia is much lower than it was a few decades ago. They have been crowded out by other species that arrived in the bay.

Snowshoe hare and moose live in rich conifer swamps over winter. Rare animals like gray wolves, lynx, and cougars hunt there. On the shoreline, aquatic insects feed fish, frogs, and turtles. Beavers eat the trees and plants of shrub thickets. Their building activity can actually turn rich conifer swamp into shrub thicket.

Beach grass grows along the shore of the bay in dunes. It helps prevent erosion by holding dunes together with its roots.

Rich conifer swamps are full of plant life. Northern white cedars and other conifers grow there. A thick layer of moss, lichen, and fern covers the ground. Shrubs like blueberries and rare orchids like lady's slippers grow in the **understory**. Northern shrub thickets are mostly full of alder. They also contain rare plants like giant horsetail and black twinberry. Dune shorelines have dune grass and sand dune willow. Wetlands can be flooded or dry. They have plants that can live in both environments. Some of these include bulrush and sedge. The threatened Pitcher's thistle and Houghton's goldenrod only exist on the Great Lakes' shorelines.

In some conifer swamps, black spruce and tamarack trees are over 100 years old.

In the water are tiny plants called phytoplankton. Phytoplankton grow in spring, along with tiny animals called zooplankton. But there is little plankton in Grand Traverse compared to other bays. In general, Grand Traverse Bay does not have much plant life. This is its natural state. It is not friendly to plants because it is oligotrophic and does not have many nutrients.

CHAPTER 4

Overgrowth of Aquatic Plants and Invasive Species

Human activity on land has changed Grand Traverse Bay. Wetlands are destroyed to make room for buildings. Hard surfaces such as concrete are installed. Rainwater cannot soak into the soil. The soil cannot filter excess nutrients like it should. Instead, water collects nutrients and other contaminants as it flows. It runs straight over the hard surfaces and into the bay. This substance-filled water is called runoff. Runoff changes the natural state of the water. It has started to allow too many aquatic plants to grow in Grand Traverse Bay.

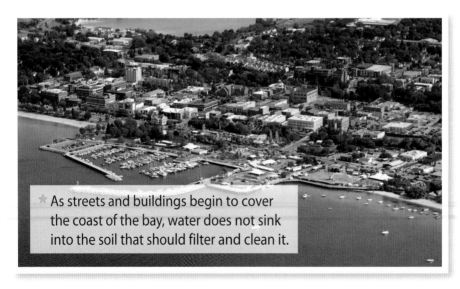

As streets and buildings begin to cover the coast of the bay, water does not sink into the soil that should filter and clean it.

The increase in cladophora seems to be linked to an increase in zebra mussels. Scientists are still learning about the connection.

Cladophora is one of the biggest problem-algaes in the bay. Huge mats of cladophora wash up on the bay's shore. Much more cladophora has grown in the past 20 years. The growth is mainly near land. This makes scientists think it is caused by nutrient runoff. Cladophora creates many problems. The beds stink as they dry on shore. They also **decay** in the water, causing a disease called avian botulism. This disease has recently killed thousands of birds around the Great Lakes and Grand Traverse Bay. Cladophora is not the only plant growing in excess. Eurasian watermilfoil is an **invasive species** that is increasing. Some types of native algae are also increasing. All of this plant growth is partly caused by runoff.

There are other reasons for the overgrowth in algae and other plants. Two types of invasive mussels have entered the bay. Mussels are a type of sea creature similar to clams. Zebra and quagga mussels are called filter feeders. When they eat, they filter nutrients and sediment out of the water. The more nutrients there are, the more they can grow. Once they filter the material from the water, the water is too clear. Too much sunlight reaches the bottom. Plants like algae grow more than they should.

Zebra mussels, named for the stripe on their shells, probably arrived in the Great Lakes from European ships in the 1980s.

Invasive species have not caused as much harm to Grand Traverse Bay as they have to other parts of Lake Michigan. But new species are arriving. One invasive fish is the sea lamprey. This fish attaches its mouth to other fish. It sucks out blood and body tissue. Lampreys can kill huge populations of lake trout and other large fish. This allows a huge growth in smaller fish such as alewives. The biosphere's balance changes as a result.

* The mouth of the sea lamprey is filled with razor-sharp teeth and a tongue that can scrape through fish scales.

* In its native habitat, the sea lamprey does not kill the fish it attaches to, but in Lake Michigan it can kill up to 40 pounds (18 kilograms) of fish over its life span.

CHAPTER 5

Humans and the Bay

Traverse City is on the shore of Grand Traverse Bay. The city was named after the bay. It was settled by Americans in 1847. Americans began moving through the area when the Erie Canal opened in 1825. The canal allowed water travel between Chicago, Illinois, and Buffalo, New York. More people traveled through Michigan. The Ojibwe and Ottawa tribes also lived in that area. These tribes survived by hunting, fishing, gathering, and raising crops. They did not damage the land. The new settlers cut trees in ancient forests. They sold the wood for construction and fuel. Logging was the main local **industry** for a long time. In the early 1900s, people realized there were not enough trees left. Fishing and agriculture are also important to Grand Traverse Bay. The area is famous for growing many delicious cherries and other fruit. The Grand Traverse region is known as the "cherry capital of the world."

★ Michigan's first cherry orchard was planted in the Traverse Bay region in 1852.

$4.00

Michigan now grows about 75 percent of the tart cherries in the United States.

Grand Traverse Bay's human population is not very large. Only about 15,000 people live in Traverse City. But it is growing quickly. Grand Traverse County has seen a 280 percent increase in population since 1900. The counties of the watershed are among the fastest growing in the state. The bay region is one of the most popular tourist destinations in the Midwest. There are still not many buildings in the area. Half of its land is still forested. Water quality is still excellent. But population growth is beginning to threaten the health of the bay.

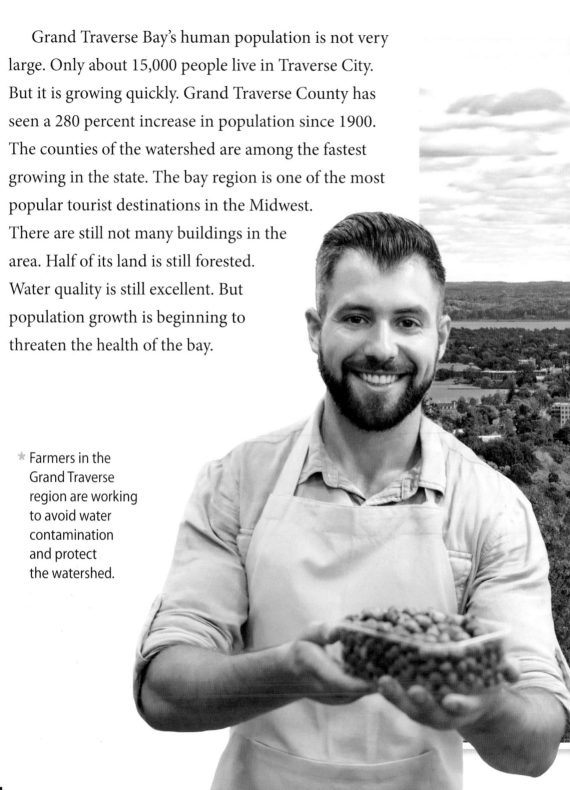

* Farmers in the Grand Traverse region are working to avoid water contamination and protect the watershed.

The area around Traverse City, which is made up of four counties, is home to 150,000 people and growing.

One threat is increasing sediment and nutrient runoff. The runoff currently present in the bay is already causing problems with plant overgrowth. It will get even worse as more wetlands are destroyed and more pavement is installed. Climate change is also an issue. Climate change has increased temperatures. This means the bay does not freeze over for as long each year. By 1993, the bay froze an average of 12 days later than it had in 1851. The ice broke up an average of 19 days earlier each spring. There are more and more years where the bay doesn't freeze at all. Without ice, more water **evaporates**. Also, some fish rely on ice to lay eggs. Warming temperatures will change the entire bay.

While parts of the bay often freeze, the bay has only completely frozen over six times during the 21st century.

What Can YOU Do for the Bay?

One of the biggest threats to Grand Traverse Bay is stormwater runoff. Stormwater runoff is rain or melted snow that runs into streams and rivers. It mixes with oil, chemicals, and bacteria on the ground. Both wastewater and storm runoff carry pollutants into the bay. Beaches in Grand Traverse Bay have been closed in the past due to harmful levels of bacteria like E. Coli, caused by runoff. To prevent dangerous pollutants from entering the bay, people can use stones or pavers instead of solid cement to build walkways and driveways. This allows water to drain into the soil to be filtered before it reaches the bay. People can also plant rain gardens, which help trap and filter stormwater.

State and local groups have begun to fix some of these problems. They are trying to reduce runoff. To do this, they build areas that can absorb and filter water. Some examples are rain gardens, absorbent pavement, and human-made wetlands. People have also started restoring natural wetlands, sometimes by removing dams. When dams are removed, fish can pass through as they should. Fish shelter structures have been built in the Elk Lakes. This protects smaller fish that have been harmed by invasive species. A similar project added 450 tons of limestone to a reef complex in the bay. The incredible Grand Traverse Bay is still relatively pure. Human activity in the area and around the world will change this unless people do their part to protect it.

The Food Chain

Introduction

The plants and animals of Grand Traverse Bay depend on each other. Plants feed animals. Small animals feed larger animals. This is called a food web or food chain. The members of a food web can be put into a few simple groups. Producers are plants. They are the first link on the chain. Herbivores are plant-eating animals. Carnivores are animals who eat other animals. Large carnivores also eat other carnivores.

In this activity you will create a simple food chain. You will also imagine different situations where the food chain changes. This will help you understand the many connections between the plants and animals of Grand Traverse Bay.

Materials:

* Pencil or crayons
* Several sheets of paper
* Scissors (have an adult help you with these)

Part 1: The Chain

First, draw four shapes on a single sheet of paper. Draw a triangle, a rectangle, a circle, and a square. Cut out each shape. Write the word "carnivore" on the square. Write the word "herbivore" on the triangle. Write the word "producer" on the circle. Write the words "large carnivore" on the rectangle. Place the four shapes on a sheet of drawing paper. Put them in an order that forms a food chain. Draw arrows between the shapes to show what each member eats.

On another sheet of paper, write a list of animals and plants from Grand Traverse Bay. Put each one under a heading for carnivore, herbivore, producer, and large carnivore. You may have to do some research online to find out what an animal eats. Now, label your shapes again with the name of a Grand Traverse Bay animal or plant and what it eats or is eaten by.

Part 2: Situations

Imagine that avian botulism kills many of your herbivore or carnivore birds (choose one species). Remove the square or triangle from their chain. What happens to small fish or small plants? What happens to the rest of the food chain?

Imagine that nutrient-filled runoff reduces or increases the population of one of your producers. Remove or change the name of your circle. What happens to the herbivores? What about the carnivores?

Glossary

atmosphere *(AT-muhs-feer)* part of the planet made of air

biosphere *(BYE-oh-sfeer)* part of the planet made of living things

conifer *(KAHN-ih-fur)* evergreen tree with needles and cones

contaminants *(kuhn-TAM-ih-nints)* substance that poisons or pollutes something else, often water or air

crop *(KRAHP)* plants grown for food

decay *(dih-KAY)* to rot or decompose, with the help of bacteria

densities *(DEN-sih-teez)* amount of space something takes up in relation to its mass

evaporates *(ee-VAP-oh-rayts)* turns from liquid to gas

food web *(FOOD web)* plants and animals that are linked together by what they eat

geosphere *(JEE-oh-sfeer)* part of the planet made of solid ground

glaciers *(GLAY-shurz)* huge areas of very thick ice that flow slowly over land

hydrosphere *(HYE-droh-sfeer)* part of the planet made of water

industry *(IN-duhs-tree)* production of goods to sell

invasive species *(in-VAY-siv SPEE-sheez)* plants or animals that are not native to an area and cause harm to other species in that area

mainland *(MAYN-land)* the largest piece of land that's part of a region or country

nutrients *(NOO-tree-ints)* important chemicals that are necessary for all living things

oxygen *(AHX-ih-jin)* the most common element on Earth, necessary for all living things

peninsula *(peh-NIN-suh-luh)* land that is almost entirely surrounded by water

sediment *(SED-ih-ment)* stones or sand carried in water

spawning *(SPAHN-ing)* laying eggs in water

tributaries *(TRIH-byu-tair-eez)* smaller rivers or streams that flow into larger rivers or lakes

understory *(UN-dur-stoh-ree)* layer of plants beneath the top of the trees in a forest

wetlands *(WET-lands)* land that is saturated with water, such as marshes or swamps

For More Information

Books

Heitkamp, Kristina Lyn. *The Water Cycle.* New York, NY: Britannica, 2018.

Herman, Gail. *What Is Climate Change?* New York, NY: Penguin, 2018.

Schram, Stephen T. *A Great Lakes Odyssey with Louis and Louise.* Waukesha, WI: Orange Hat, 2018.

Websites

Ducksters Education Site
https://www.ducksters.com/science/earth_science
Find kid-friendly information about earth science and related subjects

eSchool Today
http://eschooltoday.com/pollution/water-pollution/what-is-water-pollution.html
Learn basic facts about water pollution

The National Wildlife Federation
https://www.nwf.org/Educational-Resources/Wildlife-Guide/Wild-Places/Great-Lakes
Discover details about the Great Lakes and current threats to these bodies of water

Index

About the Author

Leah Kaminski lives in Chicago with her husband and son. She has written other books for children, about science, geography, and culture. Leah also writes poetry, often about the natural environment—so she loves learning more about everything related to science and ecology.